Writing in Cornwall

Derek, Jean & Nigel Tangye ❧ Denys Val Baker
Crosbie Garstin ❧ Mary Wesley ❧ Charles Lee
Arthur Caddick ❧ DH Lawrence ❧ Jean Stubbs
Rosamunde Pilcher ❧ JC Trewin ❧ Colin Wilson
Winston Graham ❧ Anne Treneer ❧ Jack Clemo
Daphne and Angela du Maurier ❧ AL Rowse
Joseph, Silas & Salome Hocking ❧ EV Thompson
John Betjeman ❧ Charles Causley

Michael Williams

For further information of all the titles in this series please visit:-
www.tormark.co.uk

Derek, Jean & Nigel Tangye ❧ Denys Val Baker
Crosbie Garstin ❧ Mary Wesley ❧ Charles Lee
Arthur Caddick ❧ DH Lawrence ❧ Jean Stubbs
Rosamunde Pilcher ❧ JC Trewin ❧ Colin Wilson
Winston Graham ❧ Anne Treneer ❧ Jack Clemo
Daphne and Angela du Maurier ❧ AL Rowse
Joseph, Silas & Salome Hocking ❧ EV Thompson
John Betjeman ❧ Charles Causley

Designed by Alix Wood, www.alixwood.co.uk

Published by Tor Mark, United Downs Ind Est, Redruth, Cornwall TR16 5HY
First published 2010

Photographs: Author's collection unless stated otherwise

ISBN 978 085025 421 1

Printed by R Booth Ltd, The Praze, Penryn, Cornwall TR10 8AA

Introduction

'Why Cornwall?'

The fact is Cornwall has drawn writers like a magnet. The explanation though is curiously elusive. Painters came because of the light, the brilliant, contrasting scenery, the relatively cheap cost of living. Aspiring authors may have come for all these reasons – and more.

> *Writers tend to follow paths that lead to remote places. Hero worship too plays a part; they'll go to the same places as their heroes... Cornwall, for the writer, as I see it, is like a safe area in wartime. It you want peace and quiet, this is the place.*

That was the Canadian writer Norman Levine talking to me at his St Ives home forty years ago. CC Vyvyan, Lady Clara, the travel writer, on the same subject: 'They come looking for beauty and a certain amount of solitude. The writing instinct... Cornwall seems to set it off.' The authors and poets parading these pages show rich diversity. In no way is ours a definitive line-up. But they are powerful symbols of Cornish authorship, all influenced as forces not easily defined. They were chosen over cocktail pasties and Chardonnay in our cottage at St Teath. May their appearances here encourage us to read or rediscover them. It was my good fortune to have known fourteen of the twenty-six and, in imagination, I met the other dozen.

In cricketing language, they bat in no order of merit. We merely start our tour at glorious Lamorna in the far west and travel across Cornwall, finishing at historic Launceston in the north.

I cannot write this introduction, without saluting two men, powerful influences in formative years. Charles Simpson, a painter, opened eyes and stirred a curiosity in the moors. Charles saw the beautiful and never confused it with prettiness, something quite different. He understood lines dividing past and present, fact and myth are frequently faint. Though fifty years my senior he conveyed all this: my landscape mentor.

Wallace Nichols, also based at Penzance was a vastly under-rated writer. Wallace gave great encouragement, stressing the importance of colour and character. My unpaid literary tutor, he demonstrated the tone of verbs and adverbs. The man ambled across the lawn. The girl read intently. Their spirits are surely with us as we begin our journey.

Derek Tangye, Jean Tangye & Nigel Tangye

Derek Tangye signing a book for Sarah Foot who had just interviewed him over lunch at Dorminack.

DEREK TANGYE WAS a much-loved bestselling author, his *Minack Chronicles* among the most popular books to have come out of Cornwall. The London literary agent who sent back his first manuscript *Gull on the Roof* must have lived to regret it. Derek, the son of a solicitor, and brought up at Glendorgal, Porth, was a Cornishman with the air of an English gentleman – he had been educated at Harrow. His writing oozed the very spirit of West Cornwall, especially around Lamorna, a haven for painters, Carn Barges and Mount's Bay.

We met through a press interview at his remote cottage on the cliffs beyond Lamorna, a Friday afternoon in the early 60s. He agreed on the understanding he could vet the draft. In fact, he didn't alter a word. We became genuine friends, Derek a kind of mentor. To my surprise, he occasionally asked for an opinion on some facet of his writing or a forthcoming TV interview. An old Fleet Street man, he knew all about the importance of publicity and a good bottle of wine – and liked to know something about the interviewer. Over the years an army of readers and fans arrived at Dorminack. All warmly received, especially those who brought hardbacks for him to sign. While his wife Jean – Jeannie in the books – was a hostess of natural charm. When Derek was invited to be a guest on *Desert Island Discs*, she suggested they should entertain Roy Plomley to lunch at Claridges. They enjoyed their occasional visits to London, but they loved getting home – being with their animals again, devoted to their donkeys and cats.

Long before Truman Capote hit upon the idea, Derek was writing autobiography like fiction. 'The secret weapon,' he reflected 'is the close relationship between the author of a sensitive book and the reader.' You can almost see and smell the salty spray, the flowers and the potatoes. He mirrored that brilliant Lamorna light, the sea talking, the gulls calling.

Derek deserved more attention from the heavyweight critics. They failed to understand the animals in his titles were often symbolic. His authorship had layers of experience. Beyond their earlier sophisticated London life lay country living, a philosophy of simple values and pleasure in small things, an inspiration for those dreaming of freedom and peace of mind. An *Irish Times* reviewer said 'Read the Tangye books, give them, spread them. They are hope and they are beautiful.'

In that first interview he explained 'I'm a terribly slow writer, about four hundred words a day and I usually work in bursts of ten days. I sit and stare at a piece of paper, working out what I want to say, just two or three lines... this way very little rewriting is required. I try to get it down on the typewriter first go.'

Jean illustrated his books, wrote three highly acclaimed novels about hotel life and an autobiography *Meet Me At The Savoy* – she had been the press officer for the Savoy group of hotels.

Newspaper allegations that the Tangyes were Russian spies made sensational headlines in 2000; Jean had died in 1986 and Derek ten years later. Those who knew them did not believe such allegations but I could picture Derek as a double agent. He had served in MI5 during the war.

His brother Nigel Tangye versatile: writer, Royal Naval officer, hotelier, secret agent, airman, a Fellow of the Royal Geographical Society and a Cornish Bard. His *Facing The Sea*, 1974, is an absorbing read. Some of his Cornish books developed from voyages under sail in his Falmouth pilot class ketch Spray and we must not forget his short stories. *The House on the Seine*, 1959, then selling at four shillings and sixpence, is now a collector's item, John Steinbeck calling it 'a clear and convincing autobiography of the spirit...'

PS When Howard Spring died, his widow Marion gave Derek Tangye a small ornamental tiger – they had bought it in their *Guardian* days in Manchester to celebrate the publication of Howard's novel *Shabby Tiger*. He is close by as I write this tribute to my old friend. I regard that little tiger as a talisman.

Jean Tangye with their donkeys on Dorminack land.
She loved Dorminack as Scarlett O'Hara had loved Tara in *Gone with the Wind*.

Denys Val Baker

Denys Val Baker was a colourful character, living in a curious collection of homes, a cottage at Trecrom, a vicarage, sawmills and a mini castle on the cliffs were just some of them.

Denys Val Baker in a bar. He liked the atmosphere of bars and picked up ideas for his stories.

Autobiographies, novels and short stories, he enjoyed variety. He also owned and edited *The Cornish Review*. A family man, his career and life a mixture, innocence and hair-raising experiences. Many individuals who paraded through his autobiographical pages were straight from Bohemia. At one stage he planned creating Utopia on a South Sea Island, and all done – with the occasional windfall – and wolves whining at his door. He personified the freelance, Kenneth Allsop, the TV interviewer and book critic, referring to Denys's status as 'the Freedom of a stoker in Hell...'

His output was prodigious: fourteen novels, twenty-six autobiographies, twenty-three short story collections, eighteen books on general subjects, forty-three edited collections of other writers' works – and several hundred short stories. Some would say the best short story author to have come out of Cornwall. He was of Welsh descent and addicted to Cornwall: 'cliffs and cairns and moors and everywhere the booming echoes of the restless sea.'

Dining with the Val Bakers at the Old Sawmills, Golant, was an experience. Sonia and I had to walk back in the dark along the railway line to our car parked in the village. They were great company: Denys, a vegetarian and pacifist with a liking for rum, and Jess, a potter with marvellous stories and forthright views.

He gave me writing opportunities for The *Cornish Review*, one interview leading to friendship with the author James Turner who was partly responsible for us coming to live at St Teath. Denys paid half-a-guinea for each article.

An important event in his life was the acquisition of an elderly motor fishing boat called *Sanu. To Sea with Sanu*, 1967, tells how she opened up new vistas for the family, Denys beginning his first chapter: 'Where some men dream about fair women my own dreams, for many years, have focused upon boats.'

Though we became good friends, our initial contact was uncertain. I met him at his home in St Ives, a former guest house, St Christopher's, the most diffident of interviewees, surprisingly nervous. When you asked a question, he'd often say 'I've written about that in such and such a book.' Later, when we got to know one another, we'd laugh about that unpromising first meeting. He might, midway through a meal with wine, say, 'Well, Michael, what about interviewing me?'

He died in 1984; he had been living in an old mill house near St Buryan. *The Times* and The *Guardian* gave him generous obituaries. Oh, that they had reviewed his books with the same generosity. Truth is his autobiographical authorship had a special quality – spontaneous and charming like the man at the typewriter.

His funeral was held at the Truro Crematorium: no vicar, no undertaker – the coffin borne by his family – there were six children. No church music: we were greeted by Sibelius's *Finlandia* and during the service his daughter Demelza and son Stephen sang his favourite song *I Want to be Free*. Several paid tribute to the man who was their friend. At the close there was Louis Armstrong's version of *Up a Lazy River* and an invitation to go back home to St Buryan. Among the most moving moments were when Kate Baker, widow of his old writer colleague Frank, read *Epilogue*, written by Denys. It was all rather like the end of a good story.

Crosbie Garstin

Crosbie Garstin's place in Cornish literature is secure, his considerable reputation firmly established by his colourful *Penhale* trilogy. They have such visual quality you wonder why they were never turned into cinema films. First came *The Owl's House*, followed by *High Noon* and finally *The West Wind* dedicated to Norman Garstin, 'dearest of fathers, wittiest of companions, best of friends.'

The irony of the *Penhale* trilogy was he set out to write a single novel. In the original final chapter of *The Owl's House* Penhale died, but his publisher, Heinmann, telegrammed: 'Rewrite last chapter. Penhale too good a character to kill off!'

Crosbie Garstin at Lamorna Cove, an area of West Cornwall famous for its painters and writers.

There were other works, among them *The Mudlarks, The Dragon & The Lotus*, which he illustrated (he was an excellent cartoonist), *Vagabond Verses* and *Samuel Kelly, An 18th Century Seaman*, which he edited and in which he wrote five perceptive pages of introduction.

Crosbie was born in Alexandra Road, Penzance, in May 1887: his father a painter and an important pioneer of the Newlyn school, his sister Alethea a gifted painter who lived at Zennor. The tragedy is he died aged only forty-three. Further fame and fortune, books and stories surely lay ahead.

But – and it's an intriguing but – there is a theory Garstin did not die that night in a drowning incident at Salcombe. In saving the life of a young woman, he lost his own. His wife Lilian, back in Penzance, became a widow and later Mayor of the Borough. Yet his body was never found, prompting some to suggest he had vanished to start a new life elsewhere.

In 1981 I wrote about Crosbie Garstin and his demise in Devon, in a book called *Strange Happenings in Cornwall*. Was it all over? Or was there a new beginning?

Later a reader, the Rev David Dewey of Enfield, Middlesex, wrote to me:

In 1960 I worked for a short time in the office of a London firm. There was already a Mr Garstin employed there. He was a Roman Catholic, a pipe-smoker, had served in World War 1, where he won a commission in the field... he told me he had been an author and had written under the names of Crosbie Garstin, John Garstin and Norman Leslie. Under the latter name he had published whodunits. About that time I found in my local library a book entitled The Owl's House *by Crosbie Garstin. I mentioned this discovery to Mr Garstin who acknowledged his authorship of the book. He seemed a man of good upbringing, although a rather sad and lonely figure. He spoke once of no longer having a home of his own; indeed he was living in rooms in Clapham... a man in his seventies... and he wore beautiful expensive shoes, a legacy of his more prosperous days. Not the kind of shoes you'd expect a clerk to be wearing.*

So what kind of man was he? Here is Colonel JH Williams 'Elephant Bill' recalling him 'No man affected my life more. He instilled in me, as a boy, the spirit of wanderlust and of going places and doing things.'

Mary Wesley

Between 1983 and 1997, Mary Wesley wrote ten hugely successful novels. The astonishing fact is she was seventy years old when her first novel *Jumping The Queue* was launched. She crafted her fiction with great style, plots full of guile and wit. Mary was descended from the first Lord Wellesley – hence her nom de plume – but a combination of elopement and sex clouded the family link.

Great houses are often at the heart of fiction: Daphne du Maurier's Manderley in *Rebecca*, Miss Marple, Poirot and Hastings all visiting grand residences hunting for clues in Agatha Christie's murder mysteries. The real-life Mary Wesley, an insecure young woman, made friends with the Bohemian Paynter family who lived near St Buryan. Miranda Seymour reviewing the biography *Wild Mary, a Life of Mary Wesley* by Patrick Marnham, 2006, had this to say: Mary 'took their rambling house in Cornwall for a substitute home. Colonel Paynter, a randy old widower, brought dancing girls from the Windmill Theatre down for weekends and his daughter Betty competed with Wesley to see which of them could break hearts faster. Calypso, in *The Camomile Lawn* was based on Betty, especially in her determination to bag a rich husband.'

The distinguished grey-haired lady author of the 1990s had been a stunning, spirited beauty with soulful eyes in the 1920s, straight out of Noel Coward – and I have seen a photograph of Mary rowing off Boskenna – the novels growing out of her passionate, hectic life.

She had no formal education but spoke several languages. She had lived, for phases, in Italy, Germany and France and worked in an antique shop and for MI5 in the last war, breaking German codes.

I met her just once in a Totnes bookshop – she was living in the old town – and said 'The Times has asked me to write an article about my destination for a favourite weekend.' London perhaps? Or Paris? Or Venice? 'No,' she replied 'It has to be at Penzance in your lovely Cornwall, staying at The Abbey Hotel overlooking Holmans' dry dock with St Michael's Mount in the distance. I love The Abbey and it's beautifully run by Jean Shrimpton.' Even in a brief meeting, you recognised the 'Camomile' girl, her magnetism still strong.

Mary was asked by her publisher to write her autobiography. But she declined.

Charles Lee

'I remember the delight, faintly tinged with envy, with which I first read Charles Lee. As a piece of writing in prose clear and turnable, I had to admire every page.' That was Q's assessment. Nobody has written dialect tales better, his sharp ears picking up the nuances of Cornish chat. 'He don't miss much' as Ken Phillipps put it.

Between 1896 and 1911 Charles Lee produced five novels and a range of short stories. Then suddenly he stopped writing. Was he, like Hardy, sensitive to criticism? His last novel *Dorinda's Birthday* had received some poor reviews. Thereafter he worked for JM Dent, the London publisher, proof reading, becoming senior editor.

Today the short story has gone out of fashion but, thanks to Giss 'On Books of Linkinhorne, his work has reappeared. *Chasing Tales*, the *Lost Stories of Charles Lee*, 2002, contains a biography by Simon Parker, an account of the part he played in the lives of the Newlyn School of Painters, and a thoughtful foreword by Eric Richards, a West Cornwall doctor.

Fairies crop up in a good deal of Cornish folklore and Charles Lee wove them into his fiction. His story *Wisht Wood*, published inside *Our Little Town*, 1909, is a classic.

Here is how he describes the preacher and the farming folk encountering the little people in Wisht Wood:

At first to their sun-dazzled eyes the green twilight seemed studded with innumerable clusters of scarlet berries, on the trees, on the bushes, on the rocks, everywhere. When they saw more clearly, they perceived that what they had taken for berries were little red caps, such as the pisky-ambassador wore; and under each cap was a pair of eyes no bigger than a bush-sparrow's, and as bright and unwinking; and the little eyes were set in little wrinkled faces. All the little faces were turned towards the preacher, and all the little eyes were taking stock of him, up and down, while the air was filled with a buzzing murmur, like the hum of mid-summer flies.

Arthur Caddick

Arthur Caddick in about 1966: the Poet Laureate of Cornish inns.
(Diana Calvert, the poet's daughter)

Arthur Caddick's *Under a Cornish Sky*, published by Scryfa in 2009, underlines the fact he is one of the best poets to have come out of the region: a Yorkshireman who fell in love with Cornwall. AP Herbert rated him 'One of the great underestimated poets of his time.' He could wear the jester's motley or the sage's gown. The Poet Laureate of Cornish inns, he had a considerable thirst. As a reader of his poems, he held his audience spellbound: a hint of the Shakespearean actor.

Derek Tangye in his *Introduction to The Call of the West* rated Caddick 'the Dylan Thomas of Cornwall... he has the gift of touching our hearts.' In his lyrical poems, he was drawn to landscape, in another mood he lampooned in the spirit of Punch: 'Much more technique is required in being a comic poet, the element of wit and satire, the element of surprise.' He and his wife Peggy with their five children lived in a tiny cottage – two up and two down – at Nancledra for many years. I dined there and saw his nude picture of a young Marilyn Monroe. His autobiography, *Laughter From Land's End*, published after his death, lives up to its title: a Bohemian from a golden era of St Ives, a legend in his lifetime – sometimes in his lunchtime - he died in 1987 and is buried in Ludgvan churchyard.

TOP PERSON TALKING

Put out my pink plastic bow, dear,
And wipe out those splashes of soup,
And spray me with the Gentleman's Eau, dear,
I wish to take wine at the Sloop.

The patrons are utterly tops, dear,
All Mayfair plonked down in the West,
Not tradesmen who keep little shops, dear,
Just Debrett and Who's Who and the Best.

By Gad! How it heartens a fella
To find finger-bowls out in the bar,
And a pedigree cat in the cellar,
And C.D. on the cellarman's car!

You'd like to trot down for a drink, dear?
Alright then, but wash both your feet,
And sling on that bra trimmed with Mink, dear,
You never know who you may meet.

The aristocrats down at the Sloop, dear.
Would never wear anything brash,
They jump through an autocrat's hoop, dear,
Like Gentry at Bath under Nash.

By Gad! This will shake the Tregenna!
I bet British Railways will droop,
And, darling, please lend me a tenner -
They're always so flush at the Sloop.

Broadsides from Bohemia Bossiney, 1973 (Diana Calvert)

DH Lawrence

David Herbert Lawrence was a literary genius, the author of twenty-six books, an artist with words. In a life coloured by controversy, he had a tempestuous love affair with Cornwall.

Charles Causley referred to 'those marvellous early Cornish chapters of DH Lawrence's *Kangaroo*' and, of course, his *Lady Chatterley's Lover* earned him immortality and, according to some, immorality. I remember copies selling quickly in Cornish bookshops in 1959.

DH Lawrence and his German wife Frieda who upset Cornish people in Zennor during the 1914 - 18 war.
(The Cornwall Centre)

When DH Lawrence lived at Porthcothan in North Cornwall, he showed his contempt for the Cornish: 'I don't like these people. They have got the souls of insects... They are afraid... I have never in my life come across such innerly selfish people.'

I have walked across Porthcothan beach and wondered what triggered such venom. At Zennor I found an answer. Talking with two local men at The Tinner's Arms, one said 'Lawrence may have been what they call an intellectual but he was an idiot, an odd man with a red beard coming into this pub, during the 1914-18 war, with his German wife. Young Cornishman dying on the battlefields in France and they'd come in ... the pair of them singing German songs and criticising the David Lloyd George government.'

'And it wasn't only that,' said the other Cornishman. 'He had this passion for Zennor farmer William Henry Hockin. You can imagine what the Methodists thought about that.'

In 1970 my wife Sonia and I had the privilege of visiting his Zennor cottage. Higher Tregarthen, down in a dip below Eagle's Nest; he rented it, £5 a year. I stood there and thought of when Lawrence chased his wife Frieda, scattering furniture as he went, shouting 'I'll kill her! I'll kill her!' We can only guess how their friends, the Murrys, reacted. On another occasion, DHL assuming a quarrel over, Frieda, from the rear, smashed an earthenware plate over his skull: 'Like a woman... when the quarrel was over and from behind.'

DH Lawrence saw Cornwall as a region apart: 'It is not England. It is bare and elemental, Tristan's land.' Would his response to the Cornish in peace time have been different? As it was, he was ordered to report to Bodmin for a medical examination. The two days and two nights in the Barracks there were a nightmare. He was made to sweep the floors and to be in his bed by nine in the evening. Being made to line up with other men and weighed in his shirt like sheep sickened him. The doctors turned him down, weak lungs. Those two days finding their way into a later novel.

Higher Tregarthen at Zennor where the Lawrences lived a tempestuous chapter. It is today a private property.

Back in Zennor suspicion grew. Why didn't he do something for the national cause? Lights signalling out to sea at night? A German submarine sighted off the coast?

The Lawrences' mail was withheld, scrutinised. Later soldiers searched the cottage. A posse appeared, a young Army officer, the friendly local policeman and two detectives. The contents of every cupboard and drawer were examined, a notebook confiscated. The officer set seal, by presenting an expulsion order: the Lawrences were to leave Cornwall within three days without explanation. The end to a sombre Cornish chapter.

Rosamunde Pilcher

Rosamunde Pilcher OBE was born at Lelant in 1924 and received an important part of her education at St Clare's, a girls' public school in Penzance. She began writing at the age of seven and had her first short story accepted when she was only eighteen.

Initially she regarded writing as a refuge from her daily pattern and believed it saved her marriage. She wrote nine novels for Mills & Boon under the pen name of Jane Fraser. Then using her own name she produced another nineteen works of fiction. She does not regard them as love stories: '... more about human relationships.'

In 1987 she hit the big time with *The Shell Seekers*, focussing

Rosamunde Pilcher, whose *The Shell Seekers* secured her an international reputation. 'My family was brought up with the feelgood factor, ~ that's what I write about.'
(www.westcountryphotographers.com)

on Penelope Stern Keeling, an elderly lady who relives her life in flashbacks, describing every day living during World War II. The autobiographical element is so strong that Rosamunde admitted even if she died on completing the manuscript, people would have known precisely what had happened to her: '... all about things I had known and done and it encompassed the Bohemian life I have always loved.'

The Shell Seekers, book sales exceeding 5,000,000 went on to make an attractive film; Sonia and I saw the stage production at Hall for Cornwall, Truro, in 2004 with Stephanie Cole in the role of Penelope. While her 1995 novel *Coming Home* was turned into a memorable two-part mini series starring Joanna Lumley and Peter O'Toole. Rosamunde retired from authorship in 2000 but her son Robin Pilcher, a novelist, keeps up the tradition.

Her books remain good public relations for the UK, notably in Germany where many of her stories have translated into television programmes. In 2002 Rosamunde was given the British Tourism Award for the positive effect her books and their TV versions have had on the industry.

Jean Stubbs

Jean Stubbs is a friend from Lancashire. She conjures up images of Sir Neville Cardus writing about music and cricket in The *Manchester Guardian*. She lives in a 160 year-old character cottage at Nancegollan. Her novels, more than twenty, and short stories have been translated into eight languages and have been televised and adapted for radio.

Jean's fiction can be dark or golden, often a cocktail of sympathy and drama. She is an entertaining speaker, lecturer too; she has been a writer-in-residence for The Arvon Foundation. Jean has presence and you get the impression she would have made a fine actress. Her brilliant eulogy at her husband's Thanksgiving Service at Truro remains a crystal memory. Roy, in his younger days, played cricket for Praze.

Jean Stubbs, third from right, at a Bossiney authors' lunch at Tredethy Country House Hotel, Helland Bridge.

I have a dozen of her novels in my library, nearly all of them autographed. *The Witching Time*, 1998, is a special favourite. Here is how she hooks the reader, her opening: 'The candles were burning well now, pushing back the dark, creating pools of shadow beyond the refectory table...'

Her heroine Imogen Lacey, a young woman who suddenly becomes a widow, the novel unfolding, a kind of pool, different loves and fascinations coming to the surface. It's the story of a creative spirit, a maker of glorious hats, remaking her life in another place.

Once asked by a journalist 'Who, or what, apart from your family, do you care most about?' She replied 'Old friends. Old houses. The very young. The Dalai Lama. Music. Theatre. Writing of all kinds. Beauty in all people and places and things. The light at particular times and seasons. Good food, good company, good conversation. Our cats. Our cottage.'

During our Bossiney publishing years, Jean generously contributed to the list on three occasions, her *Great Houses of Cornwall*, a tour in words and pictures of seven National Trust properties is certainly one of our best half-dozen titles. 'They are different and yet they have much in common,' she wrote. 'Tendrils of kinship and friendship curl out and cling between house and house. Their people knew and visited and often married each other... They were men of vision who improved and extended their properties; public-spirited citizens who played their part as Members of Parliament and High Sheriffs...'

Jean Stubbs has lived in Cornwall since 1975 and her novel *Charades*, 1994, is an eloquent example of how she has found ideas and inspiration here: a novel about truth, relationships and the games families play. An author who can make us laugh or cry.

JC Trewin

A son of he Lizard Peninsula, JC Trewin was a versatile writer and respected London theatre critic; in Cornwall he is recalled for the quality of two books in particular: *Up from the Lizard*, 1948, and *Down to the Lion*, 1972.

The former prompted Isaac Foot, in an *Observer* review, to say 'No one but a Cornishman could have written this book, and even then no Cornishman but JC Trewin... something of Hazlitt's style.' Each sentence smoulders like touchwood, and the next catches fire by attrition.' Wherever Mr Trewin goes you have to go with him, and he makes you see things (even in Plymouth) you had never noticed before.'

His father was a sea captain who had learned his trade under sail, voyages firing young John's imagination as much as the rows of books at their home, Kynance Bay House.

Here is a taste of that second Cornish book:

'*The Lizard's Lion*, a majestic, very roughly triangular fellow from a distance, lumpishly massive when you approach him, and from near or far a lion only to the eye of faith, sits on his haunches in the green-glass water at the side of Kynance Cove.'

In 1981 he edited and wrote the *Introduction of The Westcountry Book* with a foreword by Prince Charles, the Duke of Cornwall. In it JCT whet the reader's appetite: 'So many writers, native or adopted, name upon name splendidly various. Some of the most distinguished, classical or contemporary, are in this book.' There are twenty-eight contributors: wordsmiths as different as Thomas

Hardy, Agatha Christie, Henry Williamson, Eden Philpotts and Jane Austen.

Also in my St Teath library is *London-Bodmin, an Exchange of Letters between JC Trewin and HJ Willmott*, 1950, well worth tracking down. HJ Willmott, a cultured Bodmin journalist, and stalwart of The *Cornish Guardian* for many years, gave me encouragement to contribute to the paper, first back in the late 1960s. Here is a letter from Hampstead in April 1948, John giving us insight into his religious background: 'I was bred as a Methodist and keep a deep respect for my native chapels of Cornwall. They may not be beautiful, but they were raised by faith and, very often, uncommon self-sacrifice. Today I attend services of any kind infrequently: when I do I am fidgeted by an excess of ceremonial and pomp. What I look for is a sermon of substance...'

Winston Graham

Winston Graham may have been a Lancastrian but he was as Cornish in character as Port Quin or Boconnoc. He lived at Perranporth from 1925, when he was seventeen, until 1959, a love affair with Cornwall that never ended.

It was a wise book reviewer who wrote of an early novel: '...keep an eye on young Mr Graham, for he has come to stay...'

And stay he did: the author of forty novels and a shoal of short stories, his work has been widely translated and his famous *Poldark* saga was turned into two spectacular television series, so riveting some Cornish vicars changed the times of their Sunday evening services. The stories unfold the adventure of the Poldark family and a bitter feud with Sir George Warleggan, banker and landowner – the books selling in millions around the world.

I first met Winston at a private dinner at Carlyon Bay hosted by Dr Denis Hocking, Cornwall's 'doctor of crime,' and his wife Kate. There was something of Inspector Maigret about him. A brilliant researcher, he once took a convicted safe-breaker to lunch and when writing about the boxing business he visited seedy boxing clubs in the East End, disguised in an old crumpled raincoat.

I last saw him at the du Maurier Festival in 2002, promoting his final novel *Bella Poldark*. Sitting in his wheelchair, he said 'This is the end of *Poldark* but I'm still writing, working on my memoirs. Do you think people will want to read them? I'm not so sure. A lady friend has read the first half and said "They're interesting enough, Winston, but you've not done a lot of sinning."' He smiled: 'I'm working on that.'

Winston greatly admired Angharad Rees, who played Demelza, in the *Poldark* series and told me 'Whenever I invited her to lunch at my club, my popularity leapt. Men would think up excuses to come over and speak to me.'

The most modest of characters, Winston called his autobiography *Memoirs of a Private Man*, admitting '... this is always what I wanted to be.' There are some evocative photographs including one of the author with Angharad Rees at his ninetieth birthday dinner at Balliol College, Oxford, Winston looking at his Poldark heroine.

Any portrait of Winston Graham must embrace his long and happy marriage to Jean Williamson. In his memoirs he recalled a dance with her when he said 'I can't afford to marry yet, but when I can will you marry me?' Her smiling eyes met his: 'I think I just might.' In due course they married and honeymooned on the rim of Mount's Bay at the Old Coastguard's Hotel, Mousehole and the Godolphin Arms in Marazion.

It is one of those coincidences that while writing this profile, I discovered his novel *Stephanie*. Published by Chapmans in 1992, it is vintage Winston Graham, Stephanie discovering her lover has a double life, the plot unfolding, the master craftsman conveying tension and conflict. So much so it disrupted my work for a few days: a book you simply could not put down, a reminder he is one of our finest British novelists – in the same league as Graham Greene.

As many as six of his books have been filmed for the cinema, notably *Marnie*, directed by the legendary Alfred Hitchcock. Speaking at the du Maurier Festival, Winston explained how Hitch had a fixation 'on ice-cool blondes' and during the filming of *Marnie* he followed the actress Tippi Hedren into her caravan and made advances. But Tippi rejected them and for the rest of the film Hitch, when he was on set, would say to his assistant: 'Tell that woman to do this or do that...'

One of the most handsome books ever published about Cornwall has to be *Poldark's Cornwall*, launched by Webb & Bower back in 1983, it is dedicated to the author's son and daughter Andrew and Rosamund. No other volume has quite captured the grandeur, words and pictures taking us to the very heart and soul of Cornwall: 'It was not so much a gale as a sudden storm, as if the forces of a gathering anger had been bottled up for a month and must be spent in an hour.'

The value of his books? Ann Willmore of Bookends, Fowey, says 'First editions of his first two Poldark novels are hard to find, *Ross Poldark* and *Demelza* would probably cost £150 to £200 depending on condition and a signed copy would be about £500. *Jeremy Poldark* and *Warleggan*, slightly later ones, would be a bit less say £100 and signed about £300.'

When he died in 2003 *The Times* said 'Though he enjoyed the celebrity the *Poldark* television series conferred on him, Graham who used to describe himself as "the most successful unknown novelist in England," never aspired to du Maurier's grand status.' Nevertheless the fact he was never given a knighthood rankled many. As it was, he was a Fellow of the Royal Society of Literature and awarded the OBE.

Winston's death, at the age of ninety-three, was not only the end of a distinguished literary career; those of us, who knew him, felt a bright light had gone out.

Winston Graham, second from right, and his wife Jean chatting during a break in the tv making of his *Poldark* series, at St Winnow Church.

Colin Wilson

In 1956 an unknown writer, aged twenty-four, published his first book. He recalled 'I woke up next morning to find myself famous.' The volume became a cult sensation, selling millions of copies: author Colin Wilson and *The Outsider*.

The son of a boot and shoe worker, he left school at sixteen and became a tramp doing various labouring jobs while writing that crucial first book. With very little money, he was forced to sleep out in the open at night in London and spent his days writing in the British Museum.

Dubbed one of the 'angry young men,' by Kenneth Allsop, today Colin and his wife Joy live in Gorran Haven: a house with a notice at its drive 'Visitors by appointment only.' He writes every day, including Christmas day, and lists his hobbies as music, mainly opera, and mathematics.

Colin Wilson, the most prolific author in Cornish literary history. (Joy Wilson)

It was in 1954 that the Wilsons first came to Cornwall. In his autobiography *Dreaming to Some Purpose*, 2004, he recalls: 'It was our first holiday together, curiously enough we had camped in a field that is less than half-a-mile from the house where we are now living. Cornwall delighted me; we bought Norway's *Highways and Byways in Devon and Cornwall*, and read aloud to each other legends of giants and trolls and pixies, or stories of Drake and the Spanish Armada.'

He had discovered writing as a boy of thirteen:

Carried away by the sheer pleasure of writing, as exhilarating as freewheeling downhill on a bicycle. Every day when I started writing, I felt like an explorer preparing to discover new lakes and forests and mountain ranges. I felt sorry for the other boys at school who were ignorant of this magical kingdom where I spent my evenings and weekends.

His range of authorship is incredibly wide: more than a hundred books, fiction and non-fiction, subjects including mysticism and the occult to criminology. In our publishing days, he and Joy contributed to our list on eight occasions.

Colin, perhaps more than any other writer, has established the paranormal as a serious literary theme. *The Occult*, 1970, *Beyond the Occult*, 1988, and *Afterlife*, 1985, were just three examples of his explorations into the unknown. Interestingly too when he began his researches, he did so with the attitude of a scientist, not as a committed occultist. Eventually though he became convinced, 'evidence for the paranormal is, at least, as powerful as that for the existence of atomic particles.'

Another theme is his interest in discovering and controlling his own consciousness, so that he can reach 'peak experience' at will. Here is how he describes a challenging drive back from Sheepwash in Devon:

'Concentrating my attention because I might otherwise land in the ditch generated a certain energy of attention. And when I was able to relax on the main road, all this accumulated energy made me see that everything is interesting,'

Anne Treneer

You can describe Anne Treneer in four words: 'Cornish teacher and writer.' The adjective is essential because she was as Cornish as The Dodman and Caerhays Castle. She was born in 1891, the youngest child of the schoolmaster at Caerhays and Gorran.

Her education ranged from village schools, to Lady Margaret Hall, Oxford, where she took her B.Lit, and wrote a book on Doughty (Explorer and Arabist) under whose spell she had fallen, her *Charles M Doughty* winning praise from critics like Edward Garnett and Herbert Read. But she is remembered for her *School House in the Wind*, 1944, a Cornish classic. Here are just four sentences from it:

> *There was always something to play or do on Hemmick beach. We paddled or bathed off and on all day. I learnt to swim by what must have been a process of imitation, though I can remember the boys supporting me by keeping a hand under my chin. When we were not in the water we fished in the little pools or went shrimping.*

You don't analyse such authorship, you simply bask in its warmth and Cornish light – and she must have been inspirational. In the words of a Camborne pupil she 'made the English language come alive.' So what kind of woman was she?

One man, who knew Anne and her family, is Archie Smith, of Gorran Haven, former distinguished Headmaster at St Austell and Cornish cricketing legend. 'Anne was proud to be Cornish,' he told me, 'a quaint, warm personality who made no attempt to be superior. She was something of a tom-boy riding that motorcycle of hers. 'Anne and Leslie Rowse wrote fine autobiographical books but they were two very different people. Leslie had the belief that he was a great Cornishman whereas Anne saw herself as an ordinary girl around the village. She had this love and command of the English language but liked to talk the vernacular. "How be 'ee?"'

Apart from her three volumes of autobiography, she was the author of *The Mercurial Chemist*, 1963, a biography of Sir Humphry Davy.

> *Sir Humphry Davy*
> *Abominated gravy*
> *He lived in the odium*
> *Of having discovered sodium.*

There were also poems, short stories and historical studies for various journals, including JC Trewin's *Westcountry Magazine*. Teaching over, Anne retired to Gerrans to live with her sister. She passed away in 1966: an outstanding writer, a remarkable Cornish woman, a flame which shone brightly.

Anne Treneer whose *School House in the Wind* is a classic of rural life alongside *Cider with Rosie*.

Daphne and Angela du Maurier

Daphne du Maurier adored Cornwall and found inspiration in its history, countryside and coastline. It was at high tide that her stories began: an obsession with sea and tide, waiting for it to come in and fill every rock pool and crevice. She often dressed in blue and wore ornate studded belts.

I met her several times and, during the early days of publishing, she gave encouragement and sound advice: 'Get maximum publicity for your titles and make sure they're in the shops.' She reminded me David St John Thomas, founding father of David & Charles, did a good deal of his firm's selling.

Daphne du Maurier

When you went to Menabilly, about three miles from Fowey, you knew you were at the heart of her real and imagined kingdom. As one reviewer observed: 'The great love of her life into which she poured her energy and her dreams was a house in Cornwall.' Later she lived at Kilmarth, another Rashleigh property, a one-time dower house to Menabilly with splendid views cross St Austell Bay.

Her thirty-seven books are an impressive granite tor and her death, peacefully at Kilmarth at the age of eighty-one in 1989, marked the end of a literary epoch. Dame Daphne was an all-rounder: novels and short stories, sometimes long stories as in *Not After Midnight* – and biographies. When I asked about her favourite volume, she replied 'Each book has given me pleasure but, when it's completed, the whole thing fades. Each has its phase.' She wrote rapidly, usually completing a volume inside twelve months.

In her heyday she had the looks and the vitality of an actress. The daughter of Sir Gerald du Maurier, the most distinguished actor manager of his generation – she spoke with a slight but beguiling lisp. Interestingly when Gerald died, Daphne did not attend his funeral, instead she went up to the heath and released some pigeons. As she watched the pigeons go into the sky, she imagined her father equally free. His favourite daughter, she later wrote a candid biography *Gerald* which shocked some friends.

Why did she write? 'My main objective was financial independence... One's whole life has been pretending and in writing you're pretending to be someone else, especially when you write in the first person.'

Her *Rebecca* captured the imagination of readers in a way that few other twentieth century novels have done. But the more fame and fortune her books brought her, the more reclusive she became, almost a hint of the monk. Monasteries and barracks intrigued her.

Her *Jamaica Inn*, an enthralling novel, launched in 1936, grew out of a riding trip to Bodmin Moor with Foy Quiller-Couch. They stayed at the Bolventor inn, then a temperance house; she met the Vicar of Altarnun who told weird tales about the moor – the seeds were sown.

The Loving Spirit, *Frenchman's Creek*, *The King's General*, *My Cousin Rachel*, *The House on the Strand* and *Rule Britannia* were all set in beloved Cornwall and, of course, her factual *Vanishing Cornwall* nobly photographed by her son Christian Browning, should be compulsory reading for all councillors and planning officers.

You cannot profile Daphne and not mention her significant friendship with the actress Gertrude Lawrence which – for a time – enriched her personal life and stimulated her writing. But you just hope future scribes will not blow it out of all proportion.

Nobody, outside her small circle, was aware that her sometimes passionate, violent stories reflected her own fantasy life. Behind her charm often lay emotional turbulence, the line between fantasy and reality thin.

Noel Welch, who shared a house with the painter Jeanne du Maurier, Daphne's younger sister, on Dartmoor, writing in The *Cornish Review*, 1973 observed 'Daphne believes in living each phase of her life experiencing everything, however bleak, to the full. Long ago the escape hatches were locked, the bolt holes stopped.'

Two of her short stories *The Birds* and *Don't Look Now* were translated into memorable films. She had the gift of making our flesh creep: 'Something observed, something said would sink into the hidden places of my mind, and later a story would form.'

Although overshadowed by Daphne, Angela du Maurier was a gifted author. The first-born of the three sisters, she was the last to die, aged ninety-seven in 2002. Angela wrote eleven volumes including an autobiography revealingly entitled *It's Only The Sister*. An intrepid traveller, she once said 'To fall in love with a place is as exciting as falling in love with a human being. I've done both and often.' But she never married. In 2003 Truran relaunched her autobiography and two of her novels *The Road to Leenane*, set in Ireland and *Treveryan*: 'a story of strong women and weak men, of an abiding love that breaks taboos, and dare not be declared.' An old style Tory, Angela spoke for the Conservatives in Cornwall on numerous occasions and remained true to her Anglican faith. She lived for many years at Ferryside, Bodinnick-by-Fowey, and she is buried in the beautiful churchyard at St Winnow, alongside the River Fowey.

Angela du Maurier
(The Chichester
Partnership)

AL Rowse

From the first to last, AL Rowse was a cat that walked by itself. It will be a bad day for England and a worse one for historical scholarship when there are no more like him.

That was *The Times* obituary writer in October 1997. On the same day the same newspaper devoted a leader to him entitled 'The People's Don'.

Dr AL Rowse signing. Arguably he autographed more copies of his books than any other author. (The Cornwall Centre)

Alfred Leslie Rowse, born and brought up in the china country village of Tregonissey, became a distinguished historian, autobiographer, poet and lecturer. Some, including Dr Rowse himself, would say he was the greatest Cornishman of his generation.

He knew all about the attractions of mystery in history, probably his most famous achievement was to identify the 'dark lady' in Shakespeare's Sonnets. His claim that she was Emilia Lanier, mistress of Queen Elizabeth's Lord Chamberlain, remains a matter of academic discussion.

Coming from a bucolic home, he did well to get into St Austell Grammar School but to be one of the very first working class boys elected to a scholarship at Christ Church, Oxford, at the age of seventeen, was an Everest achievement. Even with careful stewardship, the adventure would have been doomed financially but for the tactful generosity of Sir Arthur Quiller Couch and Q's friends.

Leslie Rowse's early life had been brilliantly chronicled in his two volumes of autobiography: *A Cornish Childhood*, 1942 and *A Cornishman at Oxford*, 1965. The first a work of art, and by then a don at All Souls, he declared it was the story of his struggle against circumstances. It had made him, he said, a solitary, a recluse, hating humanity for the treatment he had suffered.

I recall Derek Tangye saying 'Leslie hasn't a chip on his shoulder, he has a chunk of Cornish cliff on his shoulder.' My great-aunt Miss Mabel Williams was AL's first headmistress. Here is how he remembered her in *A Cornish Childhood*: 'a charming smile, great dignity, raven-black hair.' She, in fact, gave him his first book and inscribed it 'For dear Leslie, with love, ML Williams.' He added 'the signature almost as elaborate and self-conscious as those early signatures of Queen Elizabeth 1.'

Tony Blair might have called him 'a meritocrat,' the son of a china clay quarryman, AL's list of published works – nearly one hundred titles selling more than three million copies – reflects his energy. In his last ten years, he spent most of his time in bed reading and writing. In his heyday he had the gift of popularising history and literature, a missionary zeal.

He was made a Companion of Honour only a year before his death in 1997 at the age of ninety-three. Many Cornish people believe he deserved a knighthood or, better still, elevation to The House of Lords. Baron Rowse of Trenarren perhaps. He had twice stood unsuccessfully for Parliament, fighting elections in Cornwall for Labour. It is interesting to speculate what kind of MP he might have been. It is equally interesting to speculate about how Westminster would have reacted to him.

A bachelor who generally preferred the company of men – though he admired Jacqueline Kennedy, wife of the assassinated American President, and a publisher – there was a certain affinity with DH Lawrence: an outsider. A complex man with more than his share of critics, like Pepys though, he retained a child's sense of wonder, a crimson sunset, a favourite piece of music, the sweep of St Austell Bay. He wrote about Cornwall with depth – and feeling.

My old Newlyn friend Douglas Williams, journalist, author and Cornish Bard, has a clear memory of the great man as guest of honour at St Michael's Mount, the unveiling of a series of John Miller paintings on the history of the Mount. 'Here,' Douglas recalled, 'he was, the son of a woman who had been housemaid there, returning as a giant of his generation, swapping smiling compliments with the Dowager.'

Dr Rowse was a lecturer par excellence. Here is how he concluded a lecture, Queen Elizabeth 1 and Today, at Claysemore School, Dorset, in 1982:

Though we live – unhappily not only for us but for the world and for world peace – in the time of the dissolution of the Empire (the world was a better place when there was more of a British Empire, to maintain peace at least within its area) and to some extent the loosening of bonds within the Commonwealth, nevertheless blood is thicker than water. Such security as there is in an insecure, increasingly dangerous world is – as we have experienced in this appalling century – to be found in our kith and kin across the world: a process which we owe to the Elizabethans who set it going and which it would be wise to encourage, support and increase today.

The heir to his £1.5 million estate was his good friend David Treffry of Place, Fowey, diplomat and banker, former High Sheriff of Cornwall. By deed of variation, David Treffry, who was fighting cancer, decided the bulk of the Doctor's fortune should be shared by the Royal Institute of Cornwall and the National Trust, with Cornwall Heritage Trust also benefiting. So two eminent Cornishmen, in their different ways, ensured Cornwall was the real inheritor: generosity of spirit.

Jack Clemo

Jack Clemo was unique. No other Cornish author resembles him, a driving creative force from china clay country, a hint perhaps of Blake and Bunyan.

Jack Clemo and his wife Ruth on their wedding day at Goonamarris. (*Western Morning News*)

'This is the lunar and the lunatic landscape of the moon,' said Charles Causley, 'a weird, white world, dusted over with the colour of sex, where workers are like walking wedding cakes.' I met Jack at Goonamarris in 1963. He was living with his mother in a tiny slate-covered cottage within the shadow of Bloomdale clay dump where he was born in 1916. Beset by ill health, he eventually went blind and deaf. As he once reflected 'I suppose I've suffered as much as any modern poet but I haven't the sufferer's creed. I've seen clearly that a poet needs a faith which links him with the evangelist.'

Despite his problems, Jack believed his destiny was to marry, his marriage to Ruth transforming his literary vision and, after his mother's death, they moved to Dorset, most English of counties – Ruth's native territory. In Weymouth his work flourished, becoming gentler, visits to Italy kindling the new spirit. In the local Baptist church he enjoyed Christian fellowship and found the inner peace he had longed for.

In Cornwall we remember him as the poet of clay country, poems embodying his blend of Christian faith and mystical erotic vision.

Like Francis Thompson, Jack had enjoyed pure companionship – and literary inspiration – in the company of young girls. Psycho-analysis shattered any suspicions regarding these relationships – the verdict being strong moral control and the assessment that he possessed 'the mentality of a genius and was likely to show a taste for extreme simplicity which would be misunderstood by average adults.'

I asked him how his native industrial terrain had influenced him and his authorship.

The china clay landscape gave me exactly the kind of images I needed in presenting my ideas of religion and sex. It is too artificial to be of much value to those who want to develop a pagan philosophy. The constant blasting and excavating suggested to me the violent Christian attack on complacent natural processes, while the stiff white breasts and clay beds reminded me of a rare kind of sexuality, different from that of the farms and woods. The element of fantasy; the almost fairy-land effects of the weird shapes and the various lights after nightfall, were all so very potent in stirring and moulding my imagination.

Considering his earlier problems, Jack has left a legacy of quality, not quantity: two volumes of autobiography *Confessions of a Rebel*, 1949, and *The Marriage of a Rebel*, 1980, three novels and a rich harvest of poetry. His third novel *The Clay Kiln*, published in 2000, is edited by Donald Rawe. Jack Clemo defined the true poet as 'an interpreter and a priest detached as an artist from the obvious aspects of religious truth, but illuminating them from a unique angle of personal vision... I dislike technical experiments which merely dazzle readers from a working philosophy instead of helping them to understand the deeper meanings of life.'

The Hockings: Joseph, Silas & Salome

The Hockings, Joseph and Silas, with their sister Salome are important figures in the early chapters of Cornwall's rich literary heritage, all three coming from the clay kingdom. Between 1879 and 1936 Silas and Joseph produced more than two hundred works of fiction. Silas has a special niche in publishing history, his *Her Benny* the first title to sell more than million copies.

The brothers upset some Cornish Methodists by leaving the Ministry to become full-time novelists. But Jack Clemo, a cousin, said of their defection 'It was a symptom of Victorian restlessness, the growing mistrust of the pulpit, the craving for new ideas and new methods.' Their authorship may not have the Cornish colour and background of say Crosbie Garstin, theirs was fiction driven by an intermingling of the Liberal and the Nonconformist. Silas, an aspiring MP, just failed to win a seat in The Commons. Joseph's *The Spirit of the West*, 1913, evocative of West Cornwall, is a favourite novel of mine and Jack Clemo rated him 'the better storyteller.'

Salome, with only nine novels, was inevitably overshadowed. She is though the subject of a quality literary portrait Salome Hocking, *A Cornish Woman Writer*, 2004, by Gemma Goodman of Treviscoe and the University of Warwick. Through marrying a successful publisher, Salome circulated in sophisticated London circles, meeting personalities like George Bernard Shaw and Samuel Butler. Drawn to the ideas and ideals of Tolstoy – like an early Vanessa Redgrave – she became a pioneer of social change.

As Gemma Goodman puts it: 'There is a distinctive drive in Salome Hocking to present the female perspective in a male-dominated world, to give women a voice. She was a woman ahead of her time.'

The brothers, with their output and convictions, sustained the Protestants, Silas's early books and all Joseph's religious novels strengthening the faith of many readers. They wrote when most chapels had big congregations and rang with alleluias – major players in the Victorian movement which made novel reading popular and acceptable among Methodists. Here is a fragment from Joseph's pen: 'If there is a spirit world,' he has said to me; 'if death is not the end and end all, although the body dies, the man lives on, why may not people visit the scenes of their early life?'

You cannot study writers in Cornwall and ignore this talented trio from St Stephen-in-Brannel. On a cold December morning I have sat in the chapel there and felt their aura.

John Betjeman

John Betjeman was a phenomenon: poet and bestseller, his collected poems, first published in 1958, selling hundreds of thousands of copies. They called him 'the people's poet' but, as Kenneth Young wrote in his obituary in The *Sunday Telegraph*: 'He was delighted to become Poet Laureate, though he was no snob, he just preferred dining with Dukes...'

John Betjeman out walking, St Enodoc Church in the background. (Jonathan Stedall)

The best loved Poet Laureate of them all died peacefully in his sleep at Trebetherick on a Saturday morning in May 1984. He is buried at his beloved St Enodoc, with its leaning spire, alongside the graves of unknown sailors whose ships were wrecked on the Doom Bar. Sir John was an enigma: his deep but complicated love for Lady Elizabeth Cavendish while being married, his Christian faith yet fear of death. He could be the jester – or gripped by melancholy.

His poetry and prose evoke the aura of another Cornwall: of oil lamps and candles, steam engines and horse-drawn carts, of children enjoying sea and sand and only a few people exploring the moors. He was born in 1906 and first came to Cornwall as a small boy: 'we drove the seven miles from the station on a horse-brake, and there was only one car in the parish and this could not attempt the steeper hills.'

John's Shell *Guide of Cornwall*, 1933, and updated in 1964, have become classics of their genre. A master of brevity and perception: Newquay 'has vitality and vulgarity.'

A man of various roles, he was an architectural critic, social historian, conservationist, railways enthusiast, churchman, spy for the British government and humourist. But how good a poet was he? There were intellectual critics who dismissed his work as 'social verse.' Dr AL Rowse had different views: 'The essential point they miss is that Betjeman is a complete poet – the whole of life is in his poetry.'

Naturally his television appearances boosted his sales: a consummate music-hall turn, one media man reflecting 'How those funny hats added to his performance.' His media style stayed to the end. Even in his wheelchair when he was asked 'Have you any regrets, John?' He responded: 'I wish I'd had sex more often...'

He knew his churches inside out: the broad C of E, the simple Methodist chapels, the churchyards – and all the trappings of church life, hymns and cassocks, incense and gaslight, windows and pulpits. As some people went on pub crawls, John went on church crawls. When you met him out on a Sunday afternoon stroll around Port Quin, he had the air of a bishop on holiday, a man in tune with the architect Sir Ninian Comper who calculated a church 'should force you to your knees in prayer.' Here in Cornwall he had a special affection for Blisland Church, dedicated to two saints, Protus and Hyacinth: 'The effect of the church, as you enter it, is dazzling and amazing.'

Walking on Daymer Bay beach or looking across St Enodoc golf course on a day when the course is a rich green we like to think we hear his plummy voice. In the last fortnight of his life, his publisher John Murray produced *Betjeman's Cornwall*, a cocktail of poems and prose with photographs and some specially commissioned drawings by his old friend John Piper: a beautiful, evocative celebration.

EV Thompson

EV Thompson is in the premier league of historical novelists, a master of hooking his reader on the opening pages. It was back in 1977 that he made his breakthrough with a novel *Chase The Wind* set on Bodmin Moor in the 1840s. The rest is publishing history.

It's the story of copper mining booming, men who 'would not be broken by poverty or exploitation': In the author's words 'the copper ore that would make one man rich and send fifty more to a premature grave.' Central to the tale are Josh Retallick, the son of a

E V Thompson - the arrival of his latest novel, just before Christmas, is good news for the book trade and his army of readers. (*Western Morning News*)

respected miner, and Miriam Trago, the wild daughter of a drunken gypsy miner.

But before that, in Rhodesia, where he headed the country's Department of Civil Aviation Security, he had published more than two hundred short stories and then returned to the UK with the ambition of becoming a full-time writer. His earlier background included being a founder member of the 'vice squad' in the Bristol police. He went to see Denys Val Baker, author and publisher, seeking his advice. 'Forget it,' said Denys. 'Get yourself a proper job.'

Looking back, Ernest says '*Chase The Wind*, was the fulfilment of a dream. I knew I'd arrived because though I was working in a fairly lowly clerical job at Devonport, the Admiral running the dockyard invited me for sherry.'

'A few years later my then editor Lord Hardinge invited me to drinks at the House of Lords and there I was drinking with him, Lord Ted Willis, of *Z Cars* fame, and Lord Stockton, grandson of Harold Macmillan – three peers of the realm. Further confirmation I suppose, that I'd made it.'

The author of thirty-six novels – collectively a Roughtor of creativity – among his latest are *Though the Heavens May Fall*, set in Cornwall and *No Less Than the Journey* about Wesley Curnow, a young Cornish miner in the United States. Ernest and his wife Celia live in an old white-faced Cornish longhouse near North Hill, part of a country estate. We have become good literary friends and when I was in regional publishing, he contributed to our list on six occasions.

There are two EV Thompsons; the novelist and the historian, a powerful combination which makes his fiction so readable. The verbal photography of his writing makes you wonder when a film or television company will translate one of them. *The Vagrant King* and *Tomorrow is For Ever* are just two that would make enthralling drama.

Of the genesis of a novel, he reflects;

A book usually grows out of something I find of interest when I am researching. It may be an historical incident, an interesting character, newspaper report from an earlier age, or even a major historical event, especially if I feel it is one that is not particularly well known. I like to mull over the subject for a long time, usually while I am writing another novel, and reading books on the subject until I am fully convinced I have found a subject I will be happy writing about as the novel develops.

A superb example of his ability to switch from fiction to fact is *For Valour, Westcountry VCs* launched by Truran, the Cornish publisher: 'The Victoria Cross is unquestionably the most exclusive and prestigious decoration for valour in the whole of the world...'

Charles Causley

Charles Causley was one of the most important British poets of his generation: arguably the best Poet Laureate we never had. His poems Cornish in their light, full of brilliant images – rhymes and rhythms setting alight our imagination.

Charles Causeley at a St Thomas Church wedding more than forty years ago. (Jane Nancarrow)

When he died at the age of eighty-six, his The *Daily Telegraph* obituary had this to say: 'Though popular – no other living British poet of his distinction commanded so diverse a readership – he was resolutely untrendy. He belonged to a conservative counter tradition that stressed the national character of its poetry and the vital inspiration of popular forms such as folk songs, hymns and, especially, ballads – he was, in his day, probably the finest writer of ballads in English.'

A Launceston man, he was born there in 1917, left school at fourteen and worked as a clerk for the North Cornwall Building Company until the outbreak of war against Germany. It was the war – he served on the lower deck in the Royal Navy – that motivated him to write. He once recalled 'When I was a little boy I thought if I could die having written one book that would be wonderful.'

Dr Causley, a bachelor, went on to produce forty volumes of poetry and prose. In a career that covered six decades, he was made a Companion of Literature, a distinction given to just ten people at any one time; he won the Queen's Gold Medal for Poetry and was given a CBE. After the war, he taught at the local primary school and became probably the finest writer of children's poetry.

A Cornish Bard, Charles never penned or typed his memoirs, explaining 'Poetry, however unlikely its subject, theme or surface appearance, has always been to me a particular form of autobiography.' A master of lyric poems and ballads, his inspiration came from somewhere deep and he wrote quickly, under pressure, as he had done at sea in those war years. His *Collected Poems*, 1951-1997 is a rich harvest, laser-sharp recollection.

He autographed in a very personal way and I first interviewed him at his Cyprus Well home, where he played the piano with gusto. He saw no conflict between writing and teaching: 'Those children teach me as much as I teach them. A non-literary occupation is a valuable thing. You must be involved with life. I'm certain being mixed up with the business of living in a small town like Launceston helps my writing. Messages come from the GPO. The poet is really talking to himself; other people are lucky enough to overhear.'

And we must not forget his contributions to *Any Questions?* on the wireless: 'The BBC never paid very much but they gave us a jolly good dinner before we went out on air though you were allowed only one glass of wine.'

Reading his poems, we almost hear that wonderful Cornish burr:

My room is a bright glass cabin,
All Cornwall thunders at my door,
And the white ships of winter lie
In the sea-road of the moor.

(Collected Poems, 1951-1997, Macmillan 1975)

Six Cornish Favourites

Bella Poldark is not only an outstanding novel: it is a tour de force for an author in his 90s. But then Winston Graham was no ordinary author. This, the last of his saga, 2002, is about the Poldarks' youngest daughter who is determined to make her name as a singer. Bella deserves to be an enduring Cornish heroine. Will perhaps, one day, an author extend her story – as Susan Hill did so brilliantly with *Mrs de Winter*, the sequel to Rebecca?

And, of course, Daphne du Maurier's *Rebecca* has to be in the Premier League. On reading the manuscript, Norman Collins said in his report to Victor Gollancz: 'sentimental... but in a haunting, melancholy way...' A novel soaked in suspense and inner vision, set in one of the most powerful houses in literature.

EV Thompson is a favourite contemporary novelist and his latest title *Churchyard and Hawke*, 2009, is one of the most exciting to have come out of Cornwall for a long time. Amos Hawke alongside Constable Tom Churchyard, trying to foil a gang of city thieves whose audacious plan is to rob mansions owned by the Cornish gentry. A theme that would have intrigued Sir Arthur Conan Doyle and Mr Sherlock Holmes.

Q's *The Splendid Spur*, my first Cornish novel, has stood the test of time. What enthralling cinema film it would make – or drama for TV.

On to non-fiction: some poetry, Charles Causley's *Collected Poems* 1951-1997. 'This book contains all those of my poems I wish to preserve.'

Finally *The World of Minack* by Derek Tangye. A marvellous selection of favourite passages from his Minack Chronicles, words and photographs and Jean's drawings making it a collector's volume – my choice.